D0788338

Cristiano Ronaldo

Arturo Contró

English translation: Megan Benson

PowerKiDS press.

Editorial Buenas Letras™

New York

Published in 2008 by The Rosen Publishing Group, Inc.
29 East 21st Street, New York, NY 10010

First Edition
Book Design: Nelson Sa

Cataloging Data

Contró, Arturo, 1967-
  Cristiano Ronaldo / Arturo Contró; English translation: Megan Benson — 1st ed.
    p.cm. – (World Soccer Stars / Estrellas del fútbol mundial).
  Includes Index.
  ISBN: 978-1-4042-7669-7
  1. Ronaldo, Cristiano–Juvenile literature. 2. Soccer players–Biography–Juvenile literature. 3. Spanish-language materials.

Manufactured in the United States of America

Photo Credits: Cover (left) © Michael Steele/Getty Images; cover (right) © Alex Livesey/Getty Images; p. 5 © Getty Images; pp. 7, 19 © Laurence Griffiths/Getty Images; p. 9 © Antonio Cotrim/Getty Images; p. 11 © Paul Barker/Getty Images; p. 13 © Eric Estrade/Getty Images; pp. 15, 21 © Nicolas Asfouri/Getty Images; p. 17 © Junko Kimura/Getty Images.

Contents

1 Meet Cristiano Ronaldo 4

2 At the World Cup 10

3 Awards 16

Glossary 22

Resources 23

Index 24

Contenido

1 Conoce a Cristiano Ronaldo 4

2 En la Copa del Mundo 10

3 Premios 16

Glosario 22

Recursos 23

Índice 24

Cristiano Ronaldo is one of the most famous soccer players in the world. He was born in Madeira, Portugal, on February 5, 1985.

Cristiano Ronaldo es uno de los futbolistas más famosos del mundo. Cristiano Ronaldo nació en Madeira, Portugal el 5 de febrero de 1985.

Cristiano Ronaldo started playing soccer when he was nine years old. He played in a **youth league** with the team Andorinha.

A los nueve años de edad, Cristiano Ronaldo comenzó a jugar fútbol en la **liga infantil** con el equipo Andorinha.

At 17, Cristiano Ronaldo joined Sporting Lisbon, one of the best teams in Portugal. In 2002, he won the Portuguese championship with Sporting.

A los 17 años, Cristiano Ronaldo se unió a uno de los mejores equipos de Portugal, el Sporting de Lisboa. Con el Sporting, Cristiano fue campeón de Portugal en el 2002.

In 2003, Cristiano Ronaldo joined the English team Manchester United. In his first year with Manchester United, he helped the team to win the English championship.

En 2003, Cristiano Ronaldo se unió al Manchester United de Inglaterra. En su primer año con el equipo, Cristiano Ronaldo ayudó al Manchester a ganar el campeonato de Inglaterra.

In 2004, Cristiano Ronaldo played with the Portuguese national team in the **Olympic Games**, in Athens, Greece.

En 2004 Cristiano Ronaldo jugó en los **Juegos Olímpicos** de Atenas, Grecia, con la selección nacional de Portugal.

13

Cristiano Ronaldo also played with the Portuguese team in the **World Cup** Germany 2006. Soccer fans were charmed with Cristiano Ronaldo's soccer skills.

Cristiano Ronaldo también jugó en la **Copa del Mundo** Alemania 2006 con la selección de Portugal. Cristiano Ronaldo maravilló a los aficionados con su habilidad para jugar al fútbol.

Cristiano Ronaldo has won many awards. In 2007, he was named the best soccer player in England and the best Portuguese athlete.

Cristiano Ronaldo ha ganado muchos premios. En 2007, fue nombrado Mejor Jugador de la Liga de Inglaterra y Deportista del Año en Portugal.

Cristiano Ronaldo is well known for his speed and for his **dribbling** skills. It is fun to watch Cristiano Ronaldo play!

Cristiano Ronaldo es famoso por su gran velocidad y su habilidad para **driblar**. ¡Es muy divertido ver jugar a Cristiano Ronaldo!

Cristiano Ronaldo does more than just play soccer. Cristiano Ronaldo also does charity work. Here, he is giving Christmas gifts to Portuguese children.

Además de jugar fútbol, Cristiano Ronaldo también hace trabajo de caridad. Aquí, Cristiano reparte regalos de Navidad a chicos portugueses.

Glossary / Glosario

dribbling (**drib**-ling) Geting away from an opposing player with the ball by making a fast movement.

Olympic Games (oh-**lim**-pik **gaymz**) A competition held every four years for athletes from all over the world.

World Cup (**wur**-uld **kups**) A soccer tournament that takes place every four years with teams from around the world.

youth league (**yooth leeg**) A group of soccer teams for players between 13 and 18 years of age.

---

driblar escaparse de un jugador contrario con el balón haciendo un movimiento rápido con el cuerpo.

Copa del Mundo (la) Competencia de fútbol, cada 4 años, en la que juegan los mejores equipos del mundo.

Juegos Olímpicos (los) Competencia deportiva que se celebra cada 4 años para atletas de todo el mundo.

liga infantil (la) Una competencia para jugadores adolescentes.

Resources / Recursos

Books in English/Libros en inglés

Otten, Jack. Soccer. New York: PowerKids Press, 2002

Books in Spanish/Libros en español

Page, Jason. El fútbol. Minneapolis: Two-Can Publishers, 2001

Web Sites

Due to the changing nature of Internet links, The Rosen Publishing Group has developed an online list of Web sites related to the subject of this book. This site is updated regularly. Please use this link to access the list:

www.buenasletraslinks.com/ss/cronaldo

Index

A
Andorinha, 6
Athens, Greece, 12

C
charity, 20

M
Madeira, Portugal, 4
Manchester United,
        10

O
Olympic Games, 12

S
Sporting Lisbon, 8

W
World Cup, 14

Índice

A
Andorinha, 6
Atenas, Grecia, 12

C
caridad, 20
Copa del Mundo,
        14

M
Madeira, Portugal, 4
Manchester United,
        10

J
Juegos Olímpicos,
        12

S
Sporting de Lisboa,
        8